Ancient Rome

A Captivating Introduction to the Roman Republic, The Rise and Fall of the Roman Empire, and The Byzantine Empire

Free Bonus from Captivating History (Available for a Limited time)

Hi History Lovers!

Now you have a chance to join our exclusive history list so you can get your first history ebook for free as well as discounts and a potential to get more history books for free! Simply visit the link below to join.

Captivatinghistory.com/ebook

Also, make sure to follow us on:

Twitter: @Captivhistory

Facebook: Captivating History:@captivatinghistory

Contents

Introduction

The Roman civilization is probably the single most important civilization in the history of the planet. Its expansion defined Europe. Its constitution shaped societies from Russia in the east to the United States and Latin America in the west. Not even its conquerors were immune to the superior Roman culture. When at the dawn of the modern age the Ottoman Turks conquered Constantinople (the "New Rome" and the capital of the Empire from the age of Constantine the Great), they found themselves captives of its rich tradition. Their own society evolved on Roman wings. Roman law and politics would later influence the US constitution, and, finally, the most obvious descendants of the Roman establishment include the European Union and NATO alliance.

In this book, you'll learn all you need to know about Roman institutions and politics. But our focus will be on the captivating stories and curious personalities of the Roman emperors, politicians, and generals—from Romulus, Caesar, Augustus, Trajan, and Hadrian, to Constantine, Justinian, and Belisarius. Equally important (and perhaps even more interesting) are the stories of influential women—mothers, wives, and lovers, from Cleopatra and Agrippina to Theodora and Zoe with the Coal-Black Eyes—whose schemes often redirected the course of history.

Unlike other ancient societies, ancient Rome spreads over millennia—from its foundation in the eighth century BC to the fall of Constantinople in AD 1453. Its history is not uniform, and Roman constitutions evolved all the time.

We can break the lengthy timeline of Roman history into four major eras. The first one—the Roman kingdom—begins with the mythic foundation of the city and its first king, Romulus, and it ends with the murder of the last king, Tarquin the Proud, in the sixth century BC.

The second period is the remarkable Roman Republic, the sophisticated era that gave us the Gracchi brothers, Julius Caesar, and Cicero. This period was characterized by highly developed political constitutions and the notions of citizenship, but nevertheless, it fell from within, eaten by corruption and numerous affairs, as you're soon to know all about. These stories will make you recall present-day political intrigue, scandalous behavior of powerful individuals, populism, and the occasional murder. Ancient Romans used to kill each other off far too often, but they always had some convincing explanations ready to be served. The public and the personal were intermingled, and political opponents of powerful men were often presented as the enemies of the constitution.

The Romans used to write often and a lot—and not only those Romans whose job was to write, such as poets and historians. Leaders such as Julius Caesar and Marcus Aurelius wrote their memoirs on a daily basis. Thanks to the abundance of the written record, we can get a clear sense of their motives and ambitions and find out the truth about the most controversial events in history, including those that involved traitors, murderers, and spy-mistresses.

The last two periods in Roman history both fall under the "empire." The Augustan Empire, or the "Principate," had a constitution that preserved the institutions of the Republic, and the emperors were formally "first among equals." This period begins with Octavian (Augustus) and ends with a bunch of insignificant emperors who came to the throne by killing their predecessors, got killed by their successors, and were controlled by the increasingly influential "barbarian" leaders.

The final era, although the most recent one, is at the same time the most unfamiliar one and it is almost completely "Lost to the West."[i] It is called the "Dominate," and it begins with Diocletian, who divided and reformed the administration of the vast empire. Two crucial changes took place during this era. Constantine the Great moved the capital to the East and, subsequently, Christianity became the official religion of the empire.

As we'll see, the greatest and most far-reaching revolutions in the history of western civilization first occurred in the Roman world.

Chapter 1 – The Seven Kings of Seven Hills: the Foundation of Rome and Its First Rulers

The history of ancient Rome begins with a shadowy period between myth and history. The foundation legend is not very pretty, and it includes a handful of unheroic elements such as murder and rape. Its protagonists belong to the bottom of society; they were murderers, prostitutes, and all kinds of outlaws who had previously been banished from their cities.[ii]

The Foundation Myth

The story begins in the little kingdom of Alba Longa on the Italian peninsula. An evil usurper called Amulius had thrown his brother, King Numitor, from the throne and forced his daughter, Rhea Silvia, to become a virgin priestess so that there would never be anyone who claimed to be Numitor's legitimate heir. But his plan didn't work, and the priestess soon got pregnant, thanks to the ethereal phallus of the god Mars that emerged from the sacred fire.[iii] That was her side of the story, which even the first Roman historians used to take with a grain of salt, but never failed to mention.

Rhea Silvia gave birth to twins Romulus and Remus. Amulius instantly ordered for the legendary twins to be thrown into the river Tiber, but his servants left the infants on the shore. A *lupa* (Latin for female wolf or a slang expression for a prostitute) saved them from dying of hunger, and a shepherd took them home with him.

The Capitoline She-Wolf – an icon of Rome[iv]

The boys grew up, met their grandfather Numitor, and helped him to reclaim the throne of Alba Longa. Then they moved on, aiming to establish their own city. It turned out they were not such a great team. The brothers quarreled over the location of the future city. Remus insultingly jumped over the defenses that Romulus was building around Palatine—one of the famous Seven Hills of Rome. Outraged, Romulus killed the disrespectful brother and continued on his own.[v]

The First Romans

Romulus, accompanied by a handful of friends and supporters, managed to build the city, and now they needed a populace. The first king of Rome declared the city as an asylum. The first citizens were outlaws and runaways from all around the peninsula and beyond. An all-male populace couldn't have a bright future, so Romulus came up with a new cunning plan and summoned the neighboring peoples—the Sabines and the Latines—to a family festival. In the middle of the proceedings, Romulus's men captured the teenage girls and young women among the guests and took them away as their wives.

A few years later, the Sabine men came to avenge and rescue their daughters and sisters, only to find out that the women were now happy wives and mothers. They stopped the skirmish and Rome became a shared Roman-Sabine town, ruled by Romulus and the Sabine king Titus Tatius.

Tatius was murdered during a riot and, a couple of years later, Romulus disappeared during a storm. He either turned into the god Quirinus and ascended to the heavens or ended up being killed by his political opponents.[vi]

The second king of Rome was a Sabine named Numa Pompilius who established religious traditions such as the Vestal Virgins, introduced the title of Pontifex, and created the twelve-month calendar. Tullus Hostilius succeeded him. His surname was well-deserved, as he was a notorious warrior who conquered and destroyed nearby towns, including the legendary city of Alba Longa. Next kings in line were Ancus Marcius, Tarquinius Priscus ('Tarquin the Elder'), Servius Tullius ("the wisest, most fortunate and best of all Rome's kings"[vii]), and Lucius Tarquinius Superbus (Tarquin the Arrogant or Tarquin the Proud). This Tarquin was responsible for the murder of his predecessor and was known as a merciless tyrant. He ruled by fear until the people of Rome overthrew him to establish the 'free Republic of Rome' in the sixth century BC.

Chapter 2 – The Early Republic: Whole Italy is Roman

No one knows exactly how and when exactly the *res publica* (Republic) really began. Ancient historians such as Livy offered a flawless narrative of what was most likely to have been chaos. They loved to imagine that their traditional institutions went back much further than they really did.[viii]

A republic is profoundly different from a monarchy, and this wholly different form of government could not be established overnight. Rome's characteristic institutions shaped up at some point in the fifth or fourth century BC. The Romans outlined the underlying principles of Republican politics bit by bit. They defined 'what it was to be Roman' and their idea of citizenship, civil rights, and responsibilities. Somewhere during that process, Rome finally began to look 'Roman.'[ix]

The Patricians, the Plebeians, and the Conflict of Orders

Those two centuries weren't ones of peaceful prosperity. After the elimination of Tarquinius Superbus, the power came into the hands of a small number of aristocratic families collectively known as the patricians.[x] Only the members of patrician families were permitted to hold religious and political office or to be elected consuls. The patricians were wealthy and influential, but the plebeians were the vast majority. During the period between 494 and 287 BC, Rome's underprivileged citizens protested and challenged patrician supremacy.[xi]

The plebeians were not just poor people of Rome. Some of them were just as wealthy as patricians, and they required an equal share of political power. The majority of Romans supported them, hoping that the change would relieve their debts. In 494 BC, the consuls needed the army, but the soldiers—who were all plebeians—refused to come. This event is remembered as the First Secession of the Plebs. The patricians were compelled to give the plebeians the right to form the Concilium Plebis and to have their own officials—the tribunes—to protect their rights. A few years later, the first written law, the Twelve Tables, was composed. The progress was gradual and more laws came in the next few decades. Finally, wealthy plebeians had equal rights as patricians. The poor still lacked basic rights, and two more secessions of plebs took place by the end of the third century.

The patricians had to acknowledge plebeian rights, institutions, and organizations. But this was merely a surface. Tribunes rarely used the right of veto to protect the interests of the poor. They themselves were rich, and their interests were the same as those of patricians. However, the institutions of the republic, and a delicate balance of power, were formed. The Roman Republic fully developed during the next two centuries.

Military Expansion during the Early Republic: Taking Italy

The secessions of plebs were so effective because Rome was in a state of war almost all the time during this time as the Roman army fought against neighboring tribes in Italy. The first war was one of defense. Tarquinius Superbus tried to reclaim the Roman throne. He gathered the Etruscan army and attacked Rome and other cities until all of them united in the Latin League and got rid of the aggressive Etruscans. In the end, all Latin cities became a part of the Roman system. Even the Etruscans needed help from Rome when another expansionistic enemy emerged: the Gauls.

The Gaulish Celts had defeated the Roman army once. This defeat was crucial for Roman growth. Despite the considerate damage, the Romans managed to consolidate their army and economy and build massive walls to prevent anyone from seizing the city.[xii] Finally, Rome managed to defeat both the Etruscans (who attacked again) and the Gauls. Next were the Samnites, the Campanians, and the coalition of cities called the Latin League, which had been created not so long ago with the help of Rome. The Romans managed to turn one tribe against the other ("divide and rule"), pull the league apart, and make those cities the first Roman colonies.

The Romans gained control of most of Italy bit by bit. The last step was to conquer the Greek colonies in southern Italy, which were known as Magna Graecia ('Great Greece'). The wealthiest and most influential Greek colony was Tarentum. The Tarentines were so wealthy that they managed to hire the number one Greek general of his day, King Pyrrhus of Epirus. His army comprised 25,000 men and 20 war elephants that belonged to the Egyptian ruler Ptolemy II. Pyrrhus won a few victories, but the Romans were far more resilient. During the first half of the third century BC, all Greek cities were compelled to enter the Roman system and become *socii* (allies). Just like the Latin cities were obliged to provide troops, the Greek cities had to provide ships for the Roman army. The whole peninsula became Roman, and it was just the beginning of Roman expansion.

Chapter 3 – The Punic Wars and Mediterranean Dominance: The Middle Republic

Now that the Roman Republic dealt successfully with internal tension as well as opposition within the peninsula, it continued to grow. During the next century and a half, Rome was in the process of becoming a true Mediterranean superpower. That meant it had to fight some new enemies, including the mighty Phoenician city of Carthage in North Africa.

Carthage was founded around 800 BC by the Phoenicians, who specialized in maritime trading. The city was located on an excellent natural harbor that today belongs to the city of Tunis. Carthage had an entire trade in the western Mediterranean under its control and, if we are to believe Polybius, was 'the richest city in the world.' Its empire, at the time, comprised North Africa, Spain, Sardinia, and Sicily. Its army consisted of numerous mercenaries and an incredibly well-equipped and efficient navy. Carthage had a hold over the western Mediterranean for years, but the Romans grew stronger, and conflict was inevitable.

The First Punic War

The two forces used to be on good terms with each during the time when Rome had to fight Pyrrhus's aggression. However, after he was defeated, Rome ended up much stronger, and its activities spread to Sicily, which was still under Carthaginian control. In 264 BC, Rome allied with Syracusan Greeks against Carthage, and the First Punic War began.

For centuries Carthage fought against the Syracusans and other Greeks to achieve dominance. But then a band of Italian mercenaries called *the sons of Mars* (*Mamertines*) conquered the Sicilian city of Messina and attacked both Carthaginian and Syracusan territory. The attacks started in 288 BC, and in 265 BC opposing factions within Messina asked Rome and Carthage for help. Carthage sent a fleet, but a Roman army came into Sicily and forced the Carthaginian commander to surrender the town. Syracuse joined Rome against Carthage, and thus the First Punic War began in 264 BC.

The Romans had difficulties approaching the Carthaginian territory in Sicily from land, while the superb navy of the latter started a series of attacks on the Italian coast. It was a tricky situation. Rome had the resources and, now that it was necessary, they decided to build their own navy. And so they did. In only 60 days, they created an impressive fleet. The Greek allies knew how to use the ships and quinqueremes, and the first naval action against the Carthaginians was a success.

A few years later, the Romans—who became a serious naval force almost overnight—sent an army to Africa to attack Carthage. The outcome was disastrous, but Roma was resilient and managed to build a new fleet in a short time span. The war ended in 241 with Rome as the absolute winner. Carthage was devastated both militarily and economically and was forced to pay expensive reparation costs. As for the Roman Republic, its power was now additionally confirmed.

The Second Punic War and the First Roman Military Star: Scipio Africanus

The Second Punic War started in 218 BC when the two sides had conflicting interests in Spain. The Carthaginian forces were led by the brilliant general Hannibal, one of the best military geniuses of ancient times—"always the first to attack, the last to leave the field."[xiii]

The Romans were preparing to invade Carthaginian lands in both Spain and North Africa. At the same time, Hannibal marched for the Alps, aiming to invade Italy. He had lost many men and elephants, but the Cisalpine Gauls joined him. In 218 he managed to enter Italy and won many battles during the next couple of years, including the Battle of Cannae. Hannibal also led a propaganda war and acted as a liberator of Roman allies, stating that they no longer had an obligation to provide Rome with troops or contribute to the Roman tax system. The Republican army lost over 70,000 men and several consuls (consuls led the Roman army at the time).

Rome had to change its tactics quickly. Some experienced military leaders were restored to power instead of electing new magistrates every year. Rome was recovering thanks to Fabius Maximus Cunctator ("Delayer") and Marcus Claudius Marcellus, who quickly became known as the "Shield and Sword of Rome." But the war was raging on other fronts, too, and the two Roman generals who led the army in Spain—brothers Publius and Gnaeus Cornelius Scipio—were killed in battle. Then something happened without precedent in Roman history: Publius's 24-year-old son, also named Publius Cornelius Scipio, became the head of the army. He was too young and ineligible to apply for a position of authority, but there he was—brave, efficient, and popular. Young Scipio restructured the forces in Spain, introduced new weapons, and reorganized the Roman legion. By 205, Scipio and his men had expelled the Carthaginian forces from Spain. In 202, now as the consul of Rome, Scipio defeated the

Carthaginians on their own ground in northern Africa, and he took the name Africanus.

Scipio didn't burn Carthage to the ground, but his adopted grandson, Publius Cornelius Scipio Aemilianus, did several decades later, prompted by the aggressive campaign of several elderly senators who said, *Carthago delenda est* ("Carthage must be destroyed").

Chapter 4 –Decay, Corruption, and Civil Wars: The Late Republic

The politics of the Roman Republic had a perfectly clean façade, with white togas, high rhetoric, advanced institutions, and a noble sense of virtue and justice. But under the surface, it was characterized by a lust for power and conspiracies. Publicly unknown wealthy individuals ruled from the shadows, letting their puppets do the politics in public.

By about 130 BC, the Roman Republic had the whole Mediterranean under its control and had already become the most powerful state in the ancient world and beyond. Lots of treasure had been brought to Rome, from the spoils of war to Greek artifacts (Greece had always had a special status and was much admired by the Romans). Without a major war to occupy them, the leading class of Rome was busy exercising power and influence internally, while gaining private wealth. Ambition and corruption defined those years, and civil war threatened to diminish all that had been achieved over the previous centuries. The wealthy grew wealthier, the poor became even poorer, and the traditional institutions were on the edge of destruction. The 'noble' families controlled entire political system, votes were constantly being bought, and plebeians were prevented from entering the Senate.

The Martyrs of Social Justice: the Gracchi Brothers

Two men were determined to end the injustice, and thanks to their highest patrician origin, they had the means to fight it. They were the brothers Tiberius and Gaius Sempronius Gracchus. The elder, Tiberius, put his efforts into reforming the very system that had made their families powerful, and he used all the methods available to weaken the aristocracy. He brought a law to confiscate many properties that the elite had unlawfully occupied and to distribute public land to the unemployed, but the law could not be enforced. Now the whole senatorial elite were against him, obstructed his efforts, and eventually got him killed and thrown into the river Tiber.

Tiberius's younger brother, Gaius Sempronius Gracchus, knew he was to expect a similar destiny, but he was nevertheless determined to redistribute the land to the small farmers. He ended up alone (his supporters had been killed), and the Senate decided that his death would be in Rome's best interest. So they promised that whoever brought Gaius's head would be rewarded with its weight in gold. The lucky winner who found his body (Gaius committed suicide meanwhile), first took the brain out and filled it with molten lead, so that he would receive more gold.

Marius the New Man and Sula

During the last decade of the second century BC, the Roman army needed some serious refreshment. The so-called Jugurthine War lasted for a couple of years. Rome had a more powerful army, but Numidian king Jugurtha took advantage of the corruption and ineptitude of Roman generals. Then a *new man* (novus homo) emerged in Rome. Marius became consul thanks to his abilities, not his lineage. He beat Jugurtha expeditiously, managed to deal with the German tribes that were moving into Roman Territory, and reformed the army.

Marius's military reform had profound consequences. He established a professional infantry, which consisted of men who previously had nothing. They were promised a farm at the end of their service, and because of that, they were loyal to their general, not the Senate. From that point on, Rome had private armies in the service of men wealthy enough to keep them.

Marius's long-time rival, the general Lucius Cornelius Sulla, took advantage of the new system. When the Senate requested him to give over the command over the army he had been leading, he refused, and his soldiers remained loyal to him personally. The army marched on Rome, and personal war between Sula and Marius characterized the next years.

The Triumviri: Pompeius, Crassus, and Caesar

A new generation of powerful generals emerged after Sulla's death. Three men—Gnaeus Pompeius (later known simply as Pompey), Marcus Licinius Crassus, and Gaius Julius Caesar—led their personal armies and competed for power. Sometimes they cooperated, depending on the circumstances. In the end, all of them were brutally murdered.

Pompey and Crassus could not stand each other, but they needed to work together in order to prevent the Senate from taking the armies from them. In 70 BC, they became joint consuls, but the elite obstructed their numerous plans and requests until another man joined them in 60 BC. The third man was Julius Caesar, and at the time he was the governor of Further Spain (present-day Portugal). The three generals established the First Triumvirate (the rules of three "triumviri"). The next year Caesar was elected consul, arranged things in Rome, and went to Gaul, where he was allowed to have an army. He led that army well and conquered everything from Rome to the coastlines of Atlantic and the North Sea.

While Caesar was on the go, trying to establish himself as a true Roman leader, Rome remained under the control of the tribune

Publius Clodius Pulcher. He was profoundly corrupt, and he used Caesar's funds to pay gangs of hooligans to do what they were told. Pulcher's actions included having Cicero banished from Rome, imprisoning Pompey in his own home, and seducing Caesar's wife. Pompey was influential enough to strike back and increase his authority in Rome, which would later put him at odds with Caesar.

Cicero against Catiline

Lucius Sergius Catilina (or Catiline) was a furious, bankrupt noble who had reportedly planned to liquidate Rome's elected officials, burn the Senate to the ground, and write off the debts of rich and poor alike. Everybody whose name meant something in Rome had chosen their sides and acted behind the scenes. The man who openly confronted Catiline was the famous orator, politician, and philosopher Cicero. He used his verbal artistry to assert that he had exposed Catiline's awful plan and saved the state.

Even though Catiline was a patrician, and Cicero a *new man*, the elite supported the latter, who became a consul in 62. The next year, the two men were candidates again. Cicero claimed he had a reason to be scared for his life, gave a series of speeches against his opponent, and had him banished from the city.

Catiline and his supporters gathered at the border of Rome. Meanwhile, Cicero exposed those that were still inside the city and had them killed without a proper trial—a decision that seriously damaged his political career. Only a few years later, he ended up banished from Rome. His exile was temporary, but he never managed to restore his former status.

Chapter 5 –Gaius Julius Caesar, Crossing the Rubicon, and Death that Shook the City

Ten years after the forming of the First Triumvirate, the political climate changed in Rome, Crassus was dead, and the warm friendship between Caesar and Pompey had vanished. The consul in charge in 50 BC, Gaius Marcellus, demanded Caesar's withdrawal from Gaul. This meant that Caesar would need to give up command over his army. He agreed, but with one condition—Pompey would need to surrender his command first.

Julius Caesar became a public enemy. The Senate gave Pompey the Senatus Consultum Ultimum and the power to arrest Caesar and get rid of him once for all. His prospects were poor; he could either capitulate or stay there and fight Pompey's army, which was nearly as powerful as his. None of it was an option for Caesar. In 49 BC, he led his army against Rome itself. He crossed the river Rubicon and went to Italy. This could be perceived as a war against the Republic, but there was no way back. *Iacta alea est.*

Caesar entrance to Rome was glorious. His troops overwhelmed those of Pompey easily, and he seized his city. The senators were terrified, but Caesar did not want revenge. His troops were highly disciplined. Nothing was ruined and, after the brief skirmish was over, no one got killed. Caesar's opponents were spared. The great leader was already popular, but this new generosity made his reputation even better. Caesar wasn't benevolent toward the senators only. He also canceled debts, brought Italians into the Senate, and allowed the men who had been exiled by Sulla and Pompey to return to Rome. Even Pompey's soldiers who remained in Rome were welcome to serve Caesar. Overnight, Julius Caesar became a public hero.

Caesar and Cleopatra

Pompey, now Caesar's greatest adversary, fled to Greece the very night when Caesar conquered Rome. Aiming to retake Italy, he employed Roman soldiers from border garrisons and gathered a huge army in Greece. His troops twice outnumbered Caesar's, but it wasn't enough. After several clashes between the two armies, Caesar finally beat Pompey at the Battle of Pharsalus in 48 BC. Pompey escaped to Egypt, where Pharaoh Ptolemy XIII had him killed, hoping that Caesar would reward him.

Ptolemy XIII desperately needed Caesar's support. He had been fighting for power against his sister and wife (the Ptolemies of Egypt loved to keep it in the family), Cleopatra VII. Ptolemy, as a male, was the legitimate ruler, but he was cruel and widely loathed. Cleopatra, on the other hand, was popular, but she was banished from the country. In 48 BC, she gathered an army and came from Syria to the border of Egypt. This was the situation when Caesar arrived.

Even though they were rivals, Julius Caesar was shocked by the way Pompey was murdered. He furiously marched into Alexandria and took control of the palace. Then he ordered both Ptolemy and Cleopatra to discharge their troops and meet him. Cleopatra came a bit early—the night before the appointment, hidden inside an oriental rug brought as a present to Caesar. He loved the present very much and one of the most famous romances in ancient history began.

Caesar and Cleopatra became lovers, and they would stay together until Caesar's death. A couple of years later, the couple had a son named Ptolemy Caesar, or simply Caesarion.

The Beloved Dictator

Caesar decided to return to Rome in 47 BC, right after the romantic episode. On the way back, he crushed all the remaining opponents. The last army that was still loyal to the memory of Pompey got defeated in 46 BC at the Battle of Thapsus.

The Senate declared Julius Caesar dictator for ten years. He was now the absolute ruler of the Roman world, and he was determined to be an excellent leader. It was his task to repair the damage that had been done during the previous years. He needed to restore the Republic, make the institutions work properly, settle military veterans, and reestablish law and order.

Caesar was a visionary who came up with concrete steps to return stability in the Roman world. The reforms were thorough, and he resolved some social issues that could otherwise lead to unrest. He, for instance, spared Pompey's supporters if they were willing to change sides. The unemployed who depended on the free corn dole were moved to colonies, where they could work and sustain their families. Caesar's army veterans were given land in the existing and new colonies. People empire-wide were given Roman citizenship and the right to enter the Senate. Taxes were reduced wherever it was possible. Stability returned to the Roman world.

People admired their just and capable leader, but the Senate was disappointed. Instead of operating within the Republican system, Caesar kept his army and had more power than anyone expected. Moreover, he exercised his power unrestrainedly. First, he appointed himself a consul several years in a row, and then he took over the powers of a tribune. Instead of restoring the Republican system, he was undermining it. Caesar's men filled the Senate. His word was law. Statues of himself were raised next to those of gods and kings.

His bust was on coins. On top of that, in 44 BC Caesar had himself declared Dictator Perpetuus (Dictator for Life). He felt so invincible that he dismissed his bodyguard. Caesar acted like a king and was preparing to become one by fulfilling a prophecy and defeating Parthia. The beginning of the campaign was scheduled for March 18, 44 BC.

Caesar's Death

Caesar's quiet opponents were enraged by his actions, and they knew they needed to do something quickly. A group of conspirators saw an opportunity and had Caesar stabbed at a Senate meeting on the Ides of March. The unfortunate dictator had expected an assault, but the death came by the hands of men whom he trusted, Brutus and Cassius. Brutus was his adopted son and, as such, he had no material interest from killing Caesar. The motives of the conspirators were of a different kind. The young men were deceived. They called themselves the Liberators of the Republic and expected to be celebrated for liberating Rome from the tyrant. However, they were wrong. Instead of cheering crowds, they found an empty Forum. The senators were nowhere to be seen. The public was not on the side of conspirators, and they realized they should leave the town immediately.

The conspirators against Julius Caesar had no idea that this was merely the beginning of one of the most exciting periods in Roman history, and it had nothing to do with them. Brutus and Cassius murdered one autocratic leader, but the process of transformation of the Republic into the Empire had already begun—and it was unstoppable.

Chapter 6 – The Rise of First Roman Emperor

The assassination of Julius Caesar triggered tension in Rome that almost resulted in chaos. The masses wanted revenge, and someone needed to calm them down. That someone was Caesar's loyal friend and associate, Marcus Antonius (Mark Antony). Antony was tribune in 49 BC, and he defended Caesar's interests when the Senate wanted him to discharge his army. He was also a skilled war commander, and he led parts of Caesar's army on many occasions. In the moment of Caesar's death, Antony was his fellow consul, and now he was the one in charge.

Antony organized a public funeral for the deceased dictator. People flooded the streets in a fury and burned the conspirators' homes. If they were still in Rome, they wouldn't survive that night. But they were already away. The man who helped them escape alive was, again, Mark Antony. Even though he knew very well that many of the conspiracy inspirers, including Cicero, wanted him dead too, Antony acted pragmatically and prevented the delicate situation from escalating into a catastrophe. Trying to keep everyone happy, he even gave Brutus and Cassius some land in new, distant provinces in the Roman East.

For a brief moment, it looked like Antony would succeed Caesar swiftly, but the Senate was against the idea. Moreover, Caesar had already expressed his will and named an heir. It wasn't Antony.

The Second Triumvirate

The man whom Caesar named as his heir was his nephew, Gaius Octavius Thurinus.[xiv] Octavius was attending military training in Northern Greece when he heard the news. Then he quickly changed his name to Gaius Julius Caesar Octavianus (the change was not final, as he was yet to become Augustus) and returned to Rome to claim his inheritance.

Gaius Julius Caesar Octavianus, also known as Octavian and, later, Augustus[xv]

Octavian quickly found out that Antony was buying his way to the top, using both Caesar's private treasure and public funds. The two men instantly became rivals. Assured that Octavian would eliminate him, Antony came up with a plan that enabled him to take control over the army. He made himself the governor of Gaul, where he was safely surrounded by protective troops. Octavian gathered an army too, with the help of the Senate, and went after him. But it wasn't that simple. Brutus and Cassius wanted to return to Rome, and the Senate quietly, yet efficiently, supported them. Antony wanted to attack Brutus, and Octavian did not want to defend Caesar's murderers. The Senate realized that Octavian wasn't interested in serving their interests, and they obstructed him by holding back the money he needed for the troops.

Octavian returned to Rome with his legions, made himself a consul, and sentenced all conspirators against Caesar. Then he and a loyal man named Marcus Lepidus met Antony. The situation was politically intricate, and just like Caesar and Pompey in the previous generation, Octavian and Antony started cooperating against a mutual enemy—the "liberators" and the Senate. On November 27, 43 BC, Octavian, Antony, and Lepidus went ahead and formed the Second Triumvirate, with the public goal of restoring the Republic and dealing with anyone who had any connection with Caesar's murder. Over two thousand influential men and three hundred senators, including Cicero, were killed. Even more people were banished. The rest of the Senate had less power than ever, as the "triumviri" (the three rulers, or triumvirs) controlled everything. They no longer needed the Senate's permission to hold an army or go to war. The political resistance was ended. The triumvirs ruled Italy, and each of them had control over some provinces—Octavian over Africa, Antony over Gaul, and Lepidus over Spain. Lepidus was left in charge in Italy during military campaigns, such as the one that Antony and Octavian led in 42 BC when they defeated the "liberators" in the Battle of Philippi.

The Triumvirate was now invincible from the outside. The only force that could end this form of government was one of the triumvirs themselves, and their rivalry.

After the victory at Philippi, Antony went to the east to fight some enemies and expand the empire. Octavian stayed in Rome and diminished Lepidus's influence. Then he made some serious steps toward autocracy. Octavian confiscated vast properties from many influential landowners and gave them to his retiring soldiers. The dispossessed people, led by Antony's wife Fulvia and Lucius Antonius (Antony's brother), protested and another civil war began. Antony came to settle things down in 40 BC, made a deal with Octavian, married his sister Octavia (Fulvia had died in the meantime), and promptly returned to the east. He had conquered something valuable there, and he needed to go back and take care of it. It was the affection of the Egyptian queen Cleopatra.

Antony's Eastern Mission

Antony planned to continue where Caesar had stopped—to invade Parthia and reconquer Syria and Asia Minor. But there were some unresolved issues he needed to deal with first. Antony had heard that Cleopatra—the queen of Egypt and lover of late Caesar—was financing Cassius, probably in order to keep some influence over the political situation in Rome. He went to interrogate her but got captured by her legendary irresistibleness. They met in 42 BC, and they were already living together when, in 40 BC, Antony had to return to Rome.

In Rome, Antony and Octavian split the empire among themselves. Rome, Italy, and all the territories west of Ionian Sea were under Octavian's control. Antony governed the eastern provinces. Lepidus was in charge in Africa, but he was no longer equal to the two powerful rulers of the Roman world. As soon as it was all set, in 37 BC, Antony returned to Egypt.

Completely ignoring the fact that he was formally married to Octavian's sister, he married Cleopatra. The couple had three children, to whom Antony gave incredible royal titles and power over strategically important provinces such as Syria and Armenia.

Octavian Has the Final Word

Octavian believed that Antony's behavior was outrageous. The last straw was when Octavia, Octavian's sister who was still Antony's legal wife, went to see her husband in Athens. She was treated with utmost disrespect and, upon returning to Rome, got expelled from Antony's house. Octavian decided it had been enough; he would deal with Antony and Cleopatra and take control over the entire empire.

In 31 BC, Octavian won the Battle of Actium against Antony's and Cleopatra's weakened armies. The couple fled the battlefield and, as a result, Antony lost any credibility in the eyes of his men. During that and the following year, many troops and kings changed sides, leaving Antony alone. In 30 BC, Octavian conquered Alexandria and took charge of Cleopatra's palace.

The story of Antony and Cleopatra ended theatrically. Cleopatra locked herself in her tomb, and her servants announced her death. Antony found out she was alive only after he had stabbed himself. Fatally wounded, he was taken to Cleopatra and died in her arms. The queen and her children ended up imprisoned, but she killed herself with the help of a snake. The son she had with Caesar was promptly murdered, so he could never get an opportunity to claim to be the heir of Julius Caesar.

Egypt had become the part of Octavian's Roman Empire. One era had ended and another begun, with Octavian as the ruler of most of the known world.

Chapter 7 – Early Roman Empire: Princeps Augustus and Julio-Claudian Dynasty

In 27 BC, Octavian was proclaimed *Imperator Caesar Divi Filius Augustus*, which literally means "emperor, son of the god Caesar (Caesar was deified several years earlier), the holy/revered/noble one (Augustus)." Octavian changed his name, and from that moment, he was only referred to as Augustus. Moreover, he was now the high priest (*Pontifex Maximus*) of traditional Roman religion. On coins and statues, he was often depicted as a heroic warrior of semi-divine origin. Yet, officially, he was only a *princeps*, first among citizens, and not a monarch. It was the beginning of Augustan Empire or *Principate,* a new period in Roman history that would last until late third century AD.

The Age of Augustus

Even though Augustus was effectively the sole ruler of the empire, he was very careful to maintain the illusion of the republican system. The Senate was still important, but only formally, to give legitimacy to Augustus's decisions.

The age of Augustus is commonly known as the golden age in Roman history. It was the time of peace, prosperity, social stability, and cultural renaissance. People were happy because "the soldiery he enticed with gifts, the people with corn, and all alike with the charms of peace and quiet."[xvi] A standing army was protecting the borderlines of the empire for the first time. Rome thrived. Augustus initiated a thorough reconstruction of the city, and gave it an unprecedented glory.

Most of all, Augustus paid special care to his own image. He finalized the construction of the Temple of Venus Genetrix, which had begun under Caesar. The goddess of love was identified as the divine ancestress of both Caesar and Augustus. The two men belonged to the family of Iulii, which was believed to have originated from Aeneas and his son Ascanius (also known as Iulus).

Just like Caesar, Augustus was well aware of the power of the written word, and he wanted to ensure a special place in history. While Caesar himself wrote, leaving detailed accounts of all his actions and persuasive explanations of his decisions, Augustus hired professionals to perform this task. Along with his wealthy friend Maecenas, he identified the most prominent poets and historians of his time and made sure they didn't lack for anything, as long as they worked on his historical project. Nearly all Roman literature classics were created in this cultural tide, but the special place belongs to Virgil's *Aeneid*, which glorified Augustus's divine origin more effectively than any temple.

Augustus's private life was strongly intermingled with his public appearance, and the members of his family had to abide to his sense of duty. His first wife was named Scribonnia, and with her he had his only child—his daughter Julia. Marriage had strategical importance for him. He divorced Scribonia (the reason was that he simply couldn't get along with her) and married Livia. Livia had to divorce first, too. She was the wife of one of the most powerful Augustus's political opponents: Tiberius Claudius Nero. Not only that he married her, but he also adopted their sons and raised them as princes with a strong sense of duty toward the Augustan empire.

Julia also married several times, complying with her father's wishes. First she had to marry Marcus Vipsanius Agrippa, Augustus's close friend and the military genius who enabled most of the emperor's military achievements (even during the time when he was just Octavian, one of the three triumvirs). Agrippa was terribly powerful yet totally loyal to his friend and father-in-law. Augustus hoped that this fine soldier and virtuous man would succeed him on the throne and be followed by the sons he had with Julia. That way, Augustus would establish a dynasty and all the future emperors would be of his blood. However, things didn't go as he imagined. Agrippa died, and after a while, his and Julia's sons died too. Augustus needed to make a compromise and make his adopted sons, Drusus and Tiberius, his heirs. The two men belonged to the Roman aristocratic family of Claudii. Augustus belonged to Iulii (alt. Julii), and the dynasty that he established is known as Julio-Claudian.

When even Drusus (who was seriously considered as Augustus's potential heir) died of a fall off a horse after a successful campaign, the emperor thought of choosing Drusus's son, Germanicus. He was another "Claudii," but his mother was the daughter of emperor's sister Octavia and Mark Antony. Moreover, Germanicus was the finest general of his time, a man of virtue. He was already immensely popular and would make a successful emperor. But then another, a bit more complicated, arrangement was made. Augustus would be succeeded by Tiberius, who would, in turn, adopt his nephew Germanicus and make him his own heir. The man who was least happy with this arrangement was, surprisingly, Tiberius.

The Life and Reign of Tiberius

It wasn't easy to be Augustus's son—even an adopted one. His private life was considered a public matter. Augustus picked his wife. She was named Vipsania Agrippina and was the daughter of the emperor's late friend Agrippa. After eight years, when Agrippa died, and Augustus's daughter Julia became a widow, the emperor then ordered Tiberius to divorce his wife and marry Julia. This may have looked simple to Augustus, but Tiberius truly loved Vipsania. The couple lived in loving harmony for years, and Vipsania was pregnant with the second child at the time.[xvii] The child did not survive. The marriage of Tiberius and Julia was full of scandalous affairs. Julia was so promiscuous that Augustus eventually banished her from Rome. As for Tiberius, he never got over the divorce and never ceased to love his first wife.

When Augustus died, Tiberius swiftly succeeded him. As the emperor of Rome, he was very competent. Rome was safe, cities were reconstructed, and the economy flourished. But Tiberius was a gloomy man, and eventually he lost any interest in ruling the empire. He retired and, unfortunately, delegated power to the most dishonest man, the prefect of Praetorian Guard named Sejanus. Sejanus used his influence to get rid of Tiberius's heirs: his son Drusus and the adopted son Germanicus. When Tiberius found out about these murders, he avenged them spectacularly. Maybe because of this, Tiberius became paranoid in his later years. He had many people killed—many of them entirely innocent—because they might have been traitors. Even two of Germanicus's sons were victims of the emperor's paranoia. One of his targets was a man called Gaius Asinius Gallus, whose biggest fault was that he married Vipsania Agrippina and had many sons with her. Tiberius controlled his jealousy while Vipsania was alive, but when she died, the emperor promptly made the unfortunate man a public enemy and let him die in prison.

Tiberius died an obnoxious death, and no one cared. He was poisoned and then strangled in bed. The man who organized the murder was Germanicus's third son, Caligula.

Caligula

Caligula was popular at first, thanks to his father's glory and because he reversed some of Tiberius's decisions. He permitted the people who had been banished from Rome to come home and restored public entertainments (they were costly and Tiberius was frugal, so he had canceled them).

During the first year of his reign, Caligula finished many public construction works and reduced taxes. He seemed competent, while in fact he was only spending the funds that Tiberius left in the treasury. He spent everything in less than a year, and then the problems emerged. Caligula became ruthless and had many people killed, including numerous senators and also his own mother and grandmother. He declared himself a god and enjoyed incestuous relationships with his three sisters, Agrippina, Drusilla, and Julia.

Caligula despised the ordinary people of Rome, and the people couldn't stand him. Eventually, the crowd hacked him to death during a public performance.

Caligula never named an heir and killed every potential one. For a brief moment, the Senate hoped that there would be no more emperors and that the Republic could be restored. The Praetorian Guard, however, had different plans.

Claudius

Caligula had nearly all his male relatives killed during his reign. However, he somehow spared his uncle Claudius, who had many physical handicaps and was perceived as the family idiot. Claudius was never permitted to a public office, let alone the army. But as the only one that survived, he was now the only legitimate heir to the throne. The Praetorian Guard found him and hailed him.

Claudius had spent 50 years hidden from the eyes of the public. But even though he wasn't presentable—he stammered, dribbled, and had a limp—he was extremely intelligent and well educated. Thanks to his knowledge of history, he knew he needed to reward the Praetorians generously to keep them loyal. He ended up being a considerably successful ruler, but he had a fatal weakness—the women in his life.

Claudius married four times. His fourth wife was Caligula's sister, Agrippina. Agrippina was only interested in helping her son Lucius (remembered in history as Nero) to the throne. She stood behind the conspiracies that involved killing everyone who stood in her way—including Claudius and his son, Britannicus. If only she knew what was coming, maybe she'd have thought twice about installing her underage son (it all happened before Nero's seventeenth birthday) to the throne of the Roman Empire.

Nero

Ancient sources offer contradictory accounts of the life and reign of Nero. Some sources depict this emperor as a mad egomaniac whom the people of Rome loathed so much that they celebrated when he got killed.[xviii] Other historians say that Nero was generous and popular, but he had many enemies within the Senate and elite.[xix]

Nero was the youngest emperor from the Julio-Claudian dynasty, and the last one. While his mother had greater ambitions, Nero cared about the arts, sports, and his own popularity. At the beginning of his reign, the system that had been established under Claudius worked well. There were enough funds in the treasury for Nero to raise some public buildings and distribute help to the poor, but the underage emperor did not understand measure and started overspending. Eventually, he needed to raise taxes, which initiated a series of rebellions throughout the empire—and he wasn't capable of dealing with the tough situation.

Nero, Antiquario del Palatino.[xx]

His mom wasn't of much help either. Instead of taking care of the unpleasant duties of dealing with the unhappy populace, she was trying to micromanage Nero's private life. Agrippina was on great terms with Nero's wife Octavia, and both were trying and get rid of his mistress named Poppaea. Some historians even stated that Agrippina had planned to kill her son to avoid bad publicity, but in the end, she was murdered, along with her daughter-in-law Octavia.

The most memorable anecdote about Nero was about the Great Fire of Rome, which occurred in AD 64. The damage was enormous, as many public buildings and innumerable people's homes were burned to the ground. The contemporaries blamed the emperor for setting the fire, and he blamed and persecuted the Christians. The fact is that he needed such an incident, and he was so happy about it that he danced and sang.[xxi] Now he had a fantastic opportunity to show generosity, organize reparation works, distribute charity—and he finally had some first-class land in the center of Rome for his construction projects.

Nero had all his opponents killed—even those who hadn't really presented any genuine threat—and went to Greece. The emperor declared freedom for Greece and was allowed to win the Olympics, despite his poor performance and the falling of his chariot. Then he performed at the theatre, and not one of the spectators was allowed to leave. Meanwhile, a load of grain was delivered to Greece instead of Rome, causing a great famine in the Roman capital.

Everyone was unhappy about Nero's rule; the army mutinied and eventually the Praetorians joined them. The Senate declared the emperor an enemy of Rome. Nero realized nothing could save him, and he committed suicide—in a slightly complicated way. He ordered one servant to teach him by example how to kill himself, and he needed the assistance of another. While dying, he cried, "What an artist dies in me!" ("Qualis artifex pereo!")[xxii]

Chapter 8 – The Flavian Dynasty

Nero had no children and managed to get rid of literally everyone who could ever be considered as a legitimate heir. Now that he was dead, there was no one to succeed him. The lack of heirs resulted in civil war. During the course of one year—the year of the four emperors (AD 68–69)—three emperors rose and fell. The fourth emerged, ruled for a decade, and had two sons to follow him on the throne. His name was Vespasian, and he was the founder of the Flavian dynasty.

Vespasian

Vespasian was not of aristocratic origin. His parents were equestrians (the class of wealthy non-patrician families), and he and his brother managed to get promoted to senatorial rank. Vespasian was a consul in AD 51. He was also the brilliant military commander who led the army during the Roman invasion of Britain in AD 43 and subjugation of Judaea in AD 66. Vespasian was the governor of Judaea until AD 69, when the governors of other provinces supported him and helped him defeat the current emperor (an incompetent usurper named Vitellius who brought the empire to bankruptcy). By the end of the year, the Senate acknowledged Vespasian as the emperor of Rome.

This emperor was a hard worker, and he wasn't obsessed with magnificence. He introduced many necessary reforms, including a raise in taxes. The economy of the empire recovered, and the army was genuinely loyal to him. For the ten years of his reign, he erected many public buildings, including the Colosseum. He is remembered in a bright light, perhaps because he was, just like Augustus, well aware of the power of written word. He financed and protected Suetonius and Tacitus—the historians that literally created our views on the Roman world. They served his interests while he was alive, and when he died, they described the rule of his son Titus equally favorably.

Titus

Not surprisingly, contemporary historians depicted Titus as an ideal ruler. His military career began in Judaea, where he fought the rebelled Jews along with his father. When Vespasian went to Rome and became the emperor, Titus was in charge in Judaea, where he eventually beat any resistance and destroyed the city of Jerusalem, including the Second Temple. The treasure from the temple served the Flavians in erecting splendid buildings in Rome. Suetonius and others had more than one reason to celebrate this capable man, but Jewish sources described him as a ruthless persecutor.

Vespasian clearly favored Titus against his younger brother, Domitian. Titus was soon given all important functions in the empire—he was a consul alongside his father, the prefect of Praetorian Guard, and a tribune. The public was prepared for the seamless transition and, when Vespasian died, Titus was immediately proclaimed emperor.

Titus's reign was short but effective. He got rid of the network of spies called the *delatores*, who had been responsible for conspiracy theories and many political deaths in Rome for generations. The emperor ruled competently and had never killed a political opponent or confiscated any land. But Titus came to power at a very bad moment for Rome. After only a couple of months into his reign, Mount Vesuvius erupted and turned the surrounding cities into tombs. Pompeii and Herculaneum were buried with lava and stone. In other cities, people lost everything they had. To make it even worse, the catastrophe was followed by another great fire in Rome and, finally, plague. Titus helped all victims generously and financed finding a cure for the plague. But then he suddenly fell ill and died— not of plague but rather mysteriously—and his brother might have had something to do with it.

Domitian

Domitian hadn't been included into the high politics of the empire and was mostly kept aside. However, now that both Vespasian and Titus (who only ruled for two years and died very young) were dead, he was the only man who could succeed them.

This ruler was an autocrat who cut the influence of the Senate, creating hostility between himself and the aristocracy. He estranged the historians that had served his father and brother so well. As a reaction, they loathed him and wrote that he was a ruthless and paranoid autocrat.

The fact is that Domitian ruled for 15 years and Rome was prosperous during that time. The emperor refrained from fighting expensive wars and instead focused on well-being within the empire. Follow Augustus's steps, he reinforced the border defenses and led a great restoration program. Unlike the senators and historians, the common people of Rome probably loved him. The army admired him and remained loyal to him. However, this emperor was encircled by enemies and ended up being murdered by court officials. The Senate decided to remove his name and image from official history (*damnatio memoriae*). Throughout the empire, statues and inscriptions were redone or simply smashed. The elite relieved their anger, but this project was not completed thoroughly enough. We still know about the emperor whose competent rule provided a firm ground for another century of peace and prosperity.[xxiii]

Chapter 9 - The Nerva-Antonine Dynasty

The dynasty that emerged after Domitian's death was quite an unusual one. With the exception of the first and the last emperor that belonged to this dynasty, everyone was adopted rather than biological heir to their predecessor. The five "adoptive" emperors are remembered as "the five good emperors." Machiavelli coined that phrase centuries ago. He praised the wisdom of those who chose their heirs by their competence rather than their blood, slightly overseeing the fact that those emperors had no choice, as they simply had no biological children.[xxiv]

The Nerva-Antonines ruled Rome for most of the second century AD, which was marked by overall stability, partially thanks to the fact that their predecessors, the Flavians, ruled competently, and Domitian had left a considerable surplus in the treasury.

Nerva

After Domitian's death, the Senate was once again tempted to restore the old constitution and not legitimize another emperor. But somewhere along the way, the elite began to enjoy the privileges without consequences. In times of crises, people blamed emperors, not senators. So now that the Flavians were history, the Senate and Praetorian Guard were searching for a particular kind of individual—competent and eligible, yet meek enough and without any biological heirs. They found Nerva, a long-time public official who was elected a consul at least twice in his career. Moreover, he was 65 and had no children who could make use of his emperorship.

Nerva was indeed moderate, even though some determination wouldn't have hurt him. He spent a lot of money trying to get support from the populace, but the army never accepted him. First, he had no integrity in their eyes. Also, the Praetorians wanted him to execute Domitian's murderers, which he lacked the strength to do. The situation got tense and it led to anarchy.

Nerva's reign wasn't going to last, and he needed to name an heir immediately. Neither the Senate nor the army cared whom he would love to see as his heir. It wasn't up to him. The elite had already picked the next one. Nerva officially adopted the man and, shortly after that, died of a stroke. The next on the throne was one of the most important emperors in the history of Rome.

Trajan

Trajan was a charismatic military commander from southern Spain when, in AD 96 (the year of Domitian's death and the beginning of Nerva's reign), Nerva had appointed him to control Upper Germania. It was an extremely important assignment, and it involved great responsibility. In such situations, the custom required a sacrifice. Trajan went to the temple of Jupiter to make an offering, when something unexplainable happened. According to a legend, when he made it through the crowd and opened the temple doors, the multitude of voices shouted, "Imperator!"[xxv]

Emperor Trajan[xxvi]

Trajan did not run to Rome when he found out about his adoption. He wanted to make sure everything was under his control, and first he had to take care about the army. Some of the Praetorians—those who presented the opposition against Nerva—could cause him trouble, so he sent them on special missions to keep them busy.

When the news spread that Nerva had died, it took Trajan a year to show up in the capital. He decided it was more important to go to the frontiers first because that's where the army was. Officially, he checked the borderlines to make sure they were safe from the outside enemies such as the Dacians. The truth is that he needed to establish good relations with the troops that were loyal to the memory of Domitian and never accepted Nerva.

Eventually, in the summer of AD 99, Trajan unpretentiously entered Rome. He came on foot and joined the people who expected him.

Everyone in Rome already admired Trajan and now his posture made him even more popular. His relationship with the Senate was excellent. However, he was the one who pulled all triggers. Trajan was a man of integrity and decisiveness and was described by many as an ideal ruler (*optimus princeps*).[xxvii]

There were two main things in the way Trajan led Rome that contributed to such a brilliant reputation. First, he genuinely cared about public prosperity, he helped the poor, and he raised or restored innumerable buildings, bridges, aqueducts, and public baths. Many prisoners and exiles were rehabilitated, and everyone was encouraged to be useful. It all worked perfectly, and that was not all.

The second major thing that made this emperor rise above others was his military conquests. First, he managed to deal with the Dacians (who were quite powerful at the time and produced lots of hassle) and Parthians (the enemy from the East that Caesar wanted to fight just before his death[xxviii]) for good. Then Trajan managed to expand the empire more than anyone else in the Roman history— from Scotland to the Caspian Sea.

The last days of his life Trajan spent dealing with rebellions on the east and north frontiers. Somewhere in between, he fell ill and died. Ancient historical sources are full of gossip, and some of them indicate that Trajan was homosexual and that his wife Pompeia Plotina and one of his putative lovers named Hadrian had poisoned the emperor.[xxix] We know for sure that Trajan made Hadrian his heir on his deathbed, and without any written document. The only witnesses to his will were his wife and the Praetorian Prefect Attianus—whom the aforementioned sources mention as Plotina's lover. Be as it may, the emperor was dead and the next one was ready to take the throne.

Hadrian

To avoid another civil war, the Senate and military refrained from disputing the legitimacy of adoption. Still, many senators were executed without a trial. The man who was responsible for all those murders was Prefect Attianus—the very same man who maybe poisoned Trajan. Attianus was indeed powerful, and he believed he would direct Hadrian's rule, but the emperor replaced him as soon as he realized what was happening. Hadrian then promised the Senate he'd never have someone executed based on unsupported claims again.

Hadrian started his reign dealing with rebellions on the Roman frontiers, which were so stretched that they became hard to defend. Excessive expansion of Roman territory under Trajan had only brought problems, and Hadrian decided to go in the opposite direction. Just like Augustus, he cared about stability within the existing borders, so he stopped further expansion and even gave up Armenia and Mesopotamia. Hadrian reorganized the defenses, introduced strict military discipline, and built the famous Hadrian's Wall in Britain "to separate Romans from barbarians."[xxx]

People in the provinces loved this emperor because he not only gave them a lot of autonomy, but he also built and restored many buildings in cities throughout the empire. Greeks were happy about his efforts, but the people of Judaea were not. They did not want to be assimilated into the Graeco-Roman world, so when the Romans tried to build a temple to Jupiter on the ruins of an ancient Temple in Jerusalem, the Jews raised the Bar Kokhba revolt. Many died on both sides. Hadrian's army eventually crushed the opposition, and the consequences were terrible for the Jews. This was the moment in history when they lost their lands. Hadrian renamed the province of Judaea into Palestine (the ancient name of the land of Philistines—the people that disappeared from history centuries earlier) and combined it with Syria. The new province was named Syria Palestine (or Syria Palaestina), Jerusalem became Aelia Capitolina, and the people were taken into slavery.

Hadrian was a Graecophile, a lover of Greek culture and arts—and of one particular young Greek named Antinous. Contemporary sources reveal that the emperor was so overwhelmed by his lover's premature death that he wept like a woman.^{xxxi} He, of course, had a wife, but his marriage was unhappy. Hadrian died of heart failure, and the title of Roman emperor went to his adopted son Antoninus.

Antoninus Pius

Antoninus was Hadrian's third choice—the man he intended to adopt had already died and the second one, Marcus Aurelius, was too young. Antoninus was there to close the gap, rule a couple of years, and be succeeded by Aurelius. To everyone's surprise, Antoninus ruled for 23 years, and those years were peaceful and prosperous. Because of his piety and gratefulness, he was remembered as Antoninus Pius.

Antoninus continued with Hadrian's policies, but he did it a bit differently. He was in Rome most of the time, allowing the loyal military leaders to take care of occasional conflicts on the borders. He also freed a number of men who had been imprisoned during his predecessor's reign, stating that Hadrian would have set them free them himself if he had the chance.

The frugal emperor took great care of public finances, and he could afford his many construction projects, such as the memorial temples of his wife Faustina and his benefactor Hadrian, and the impressive Antonine Wall in Scotland.

Marcus Aurelius

Antoninus Pius had two sons and many daughters with Faustina, but almost all of them predeceased him. In terms of succession, it didn't make any difference. His successors were determined more than two decades earlier. They were Marcus Aurelius and Lucius Verus. The two men ruled jointly until Verus's death, when Aurelius declared his son Commodus a co-emperor.

Aurelius was marked as last of the five good emperors by Machiavelli. Best known as a philosopher and one of the most important ideologues of stoicism, as well as the author of

Meditations, Aurelius epitomized the Platonic ideal of the philosopher king. He used his power wisely in order to help people rather than to help himself.

No matter how much he appreciated life in contemplation, this emperor was a competent war commander who spent many years on the battlefields, fighting barbarian tribes on the Danube frontier. He was just about to defeat the Parthians when he died at Vindobona in present-day Austria.

Commodus

Marcus Aurelius died in AD 180, leaving his teenage son to rule alone. It was a particularly difficult moment in history. Year after year, the enemies on the borders grew stronger. The Roman army was making a great effort to prevent an invasion. On top of that, Commodus was underage and incompetent to rule the empire.

The son of Marcus Aurelius had received the finest education possible and was expected to rule wisely. However, he turned up to be a senseless egomaniac. Commodus fought with gladiators (of course, no one was permitted to harm him) and loved to be depicted as Hercules. He let a few opportunists lead Rome and turn it into chaos. Consulships were literally sold; people were getting killed for ridiculous reasons, and the economy of the empire was in jeopardy. The emperor didn't care. Ruling the state was boring for him, and he wanted to make it more fun. His creative ideas included renaming the empire to Commodiana, executing the consuls, and replacing them with gladiators. Providentially, the Praetorian prefect found out about it and arranged for the mad emperor to be poisoned. The task was difficult. Commodus's mistress offered him a glass of poisoned wine, which he eagerly accepted. But he was already so drunk that he vomited the wine up. Poisoning was not so good idea after all, and the conspirators had to go ahead with the plan B, which was strangling the emperor to death. Commodus's personal trainer did it successfully.

Many historians have marked the period of Commodus's reign as the very moment when Rome ceased to be a highly organized society and an invincible super force and turned into a kingdom "of iron and rust."[xxxii] Many accounts of ancient Rome stop here, but this one continues. The Roman Empire did not fall in the second century AD. It lasted for hundreds of years after the reign of Commodus and was yet to see many moments of glory under some of its most visionary rulers, such as Diocletian and Constantine.

Chapter 10 – Late Empire

The Nerva-Antonine dynasty ended with the death of Commodus. A period of great uncertainty began, and it lasted for an entire century. The throne of Rome was in the hands of many usurpers who came to power by killing their predecessors. All of them ended in the same fashion: killed by the next emperor or the Praetorian Guard. Most of the third century AD remained known as the Crisis of the Third Century or the Imperial Crisis. Roman troops fought each other in order to install their generals on top of the state, while barbarian hordes hit the borders. Twenty-nine emperors rose and fell in only five decades, pushing the empire into further turmoil. Finally, one soldier-turned-emperor decided to put a stop to further decay and enable a period of stability.

Diocletian and the Tetrarchy

Just like many before him, Diocletian ended up on the throne thanks to his troops, by killing the previous emperor and crushing his army. Unlike his predecessors, he wasn't blinded by power. He understood that one man couldn't efficiently control the Roman Empire in its entirety—especially not in chaotic circumstances that characterized the third century AD. So he split it in half.

Diocletian was now in charge on the eastern (mainly Greek) part of the empire, and he gave his friend Maximian the control over the western (Latin) part. The administration worked so efficiently that the emperor came to the idea to further divide each half of the empire and establish the tetrarchy (the rule of four). Diocletian and Maximian both had the titles of Roman emperor (August), while the two new tetrarchs, called Galerius and Constantius Chlorus ("the Pale"), were given the titles of junior emperors (Caesar).

Diocletian introduced various reforms and brought order into the army, administration, and tax system. He also acknowledged that the Augustan model of empire that relied on the institutions of the republic no longer functioned. The Principate ended and the new model, called Dominate, began. The new emperor was dressed in gold, wore a crown, and was presented as the embodiment of Jupiter on Earth. Traditional Roman (pagan) religion supported this, as rulers had been deified for centuries. The populace was required to venerate Diocletian as the embodiment of Jupiter on Earth and to make ceremonial sacrifices to him.

His pagan subjects gladly followed the new rules. After all, this was the emperor who restored stability after a century of terrible conditions. But by this point, there were a significant number of Christians in the empire, and for Diocletian they meant trouble. Even though they were model citizens who served the army and paid taxes, they were persistently refusing to make a sacrifice to the emperor. For them, there was only one God, and it was not the emperor.

Angry because of this undermining of his imperial authority, Diocletian decided to terminate Christianity in the empire. Churches were demolished, writings were burned, and people were captured, banished, or killed. Neither repression nor propaganda produced the results he wanted. It was just the opposite. Christianity grew stronger than ever, and Diocletian was under such pressure that he stepped down from the throne.

When Diocletian abdicated in AD 305, his colleague had to follow his example. Both emperors retired and left their authorities to Galerius and Constantius, who, in turn, had to name new junior emperors. The trouble emerged from the fact that Constantius and

Maximian had sons. Both of them were established generals, and both were left out, while some new men got promoted to junior emperors.

The End of Tetrarchy

Compared to other tetrarchs, Constantius the Pale was the most popular one. He was honest, just, and down-to-earth. Unlike others, he never persecuted Christians or anyone else, and his army was a diverse one in terms of religion. However, he was dying. His paleness was not metaphorical—he was ill with leukemia. He died during a campaign in Britain and was mourned sincerely by his soldiers. His army was informed that they would now serve the new emperor, called Severus. Most of them had never heard of Severus. They were loyal to Constantius and his son named Constantine, who often joined his father in campaigns. The soldiers knew him, admired him—and declared him their emperor. The short-lived period of peaceful transition established under Diocletian had come to an end.

Constantine Takes the West…

Maximian's son, Maxentius, loved the idea of seizing power the way Constantine did, and so he employed the troops that used to serve his father and captured Rome. At that moment, the Roman Empire had six emperors: the four legal ones and two self-proclaimed. By AD 312, only the "illegal" ones were left in the western half of the empire.

Maxentius never intended to cooperate with Constantine. Rome and the rest of Italy were his. He had a huge army and numerous defenses. But Maxentius was a cruel and unpopular ruler, and his army did not cherish him the way Constantine's men valued their leader. So when Constantine and his forty thousand men invaded Italy, Maxentius and his troops fled the city.

The two forces met at the Milvian Bridge, and Constantine crushed his opponent. He later claimed Christ guided him. The next day, Rome got a new leader. Constantine entered the city proudly holding his opponent's head on a spear. He was now the emperor of the Western Roman Empire, and it was just the beginning for this visionary ruler.

There was something special about Constantine, something that granted him enormous popularity. He marched into Rome as a savior, rather than as an oppressor like Maxentius. He was a people's man. Furthermore, in such delicate times when Christians were oppressed throughout the empire, he picked Christ rather than Jupiter, and refused to make the customary offering to the old pagan god. But Constantine didn't just turn sides. The emperor legalized Christianity through an edict of toleration in 313, but he made sure not to alienate his pagan subjects, and did not make a new religion the official one. He has been seen ever since as a pioneer of religious toleration.

...and the East

While Constantine and Maxentius fought in the Western Empire, something similar happened in the Eastern Empire as well. Licinius—one of the legit tetrarchs at first, and now the sole ruler of the East—had already beaten his competition and had his junior emperor, Valerius Valens, killed. Constantine was his only threat, but the two emperors made a deal, and each was in charge of their own half of the empire. But quiet hostility grew to the point when conflict became inevitable.

Licinius made a fatal mistake. There were even more Christians in the eastern half of the empire than in the western, and Licinius believed they would all support Constantine. Because of that, he started persecuting his subjects. This gave a perfect opportunity for Constantine to show up as the protector of people, so he came with an army and attacked Licinius. The armies met near Byzantium, which was still just a minor Greek colony and was yet to become the center of the known universe and, naturally, Constantine won.

Chapter 11 – The Empire of Constantine

For the first time in recent history, the entire Roman Empire had a single emperor. Constantine was competent and strong enough to take on the responsibility. It wasn't easy. Frequent civil wars had destabilized the empire, and Constantine carried out a number of reforms to make everything function as it should. The economy was recovering, thanks to the fact that the working classes could work again instead of going to wars. To speed up the recuperation, Constantine locked everyone within their occupations. The farmers could not leave their land, and the members of guilds (whole families) could not change profession. Such drastic measures had a different effect in the eastern and western halves of the empire. The East was already stable and thriving, and those orders were largely ignored. In the West, however, the reforms resulted in the medieval feudal system.

Since there was no one left who could dispute his position on the throne, Constantine went a little further in fostering Christianity. First he sent his mother on the very first pilgrimage in history, during which she founded many churches, such as the Church of the Nativity in Bethlehem and the Church of the Holy Sepulchre at Golgotha in Jerusalem, and numerous hostels and hospitals along the way. The next step in promoting the new faith included the banishment of ritual sacrifice, orgies, and gladiatorial games. The practice of crucifixion also became forbidden. The only popular public spectacle that was still allowed was the chariot race because it wasn't violent.

The First Heretics: the Arians

Constantine thoroughly transformed the empire, and its link with Christianity was now unbreakable. Everything appeared sorted out when a new challenge appeared. A brilliantly persuasive young priest from Egypt started teaching his own views on Jesus Christ. The priest's name was Arius, and he believed that Christ was not a god in a true sense and that he was inferior to God the Father. Arius attracted many followers, and they remained at his side even when a new bishop was appointed to replace him in Alexandria. This situation threatened to break the church, which was still decentralized and not organized properly.

The official opinion of the church did not exist as such—and it was just about time for the church to consolidate and express its views. The future of the empire depended on it, and it was Constantine who initiated finding a permanent solution. As he was interested in social stability rather than theology, he offered simple solutions, such as working out the differences. When there was no response to his appeal, he gathered a great council in Nicaea, where he confronted all bishops in the empire. The majority decided that Arius was wrong, and he was excommunicated from the church. Thanks to Constantine, Christianity was now united, but the harmony was provisional and wasn't going to last. It didn't make any difference for the emperor, who was already preparing for one of his greatest projects.

Building Constantinople (New Rome)

Now that Constantine had dealt with the delicate issues, he decided it was time for some remarkable construction works. He made an astonishing basilica in Rome, with a large statue of himself inside, and a few other churches, including one for the pope.

Nevertheless, Constantine did not want to rule from Rome. The city was not that important strategically anymore, and it contained visible traces of degeneration and corruption. Rome was the city of the past, and Constantine imagined a city of the future. The empire had changed a lot during his reign, and he thought it deserved a new capital—a New Rome (Nova Roma).

It wasn't easy to find the perfect ground for such endeavor, but Constantine, as he later claimed, was led by divine voice. God led him to the very place where he crushed Licinius and became the emperor of both East and West: the ancient city of Byzantium.

This thousand-years-old Greek colony was sited on a perfect spot just between the eastern and western edges of the empire. Bordered on three sides with water, it had excellent natural defenses. The city's large harbor was located between the Mediterranean and the Black Sea, at the midpoint of lucrative trade routes. The place was so perfect—and later history would attest to it—that it is a true wonder why no one before Constantine had come to the idea to build a capital on that spot.

Constantine employed all available resources and the magnificent new city emerged within the period of just six years. People from all regions of the empire were glad to move to New Rome and enjoy the various benefits, such as free grain and fresh water, as well as the chance of improvement of their status.

The new capital was dedicated in AD 330. During the rule of Constantine, it was referred to as New Rome. A century later, the official name was Constantinople, and it remained so until the twentieth century when it was changed to Istanbul. In the present day, the city is the capital of Turkey.

The Last Years of Constantine the Great: A Dark Secret, Baptism, and Death

In the later period of his reign, it wasn't easy for Constantine to preserve political and religious harmony. He became an oppressive ruler and utilized severe and sometimes unjust measures to return some prosperity. He was efficient in doing so, but he also grew ruthless. He killed many who, no matter how slightly, appeared as his potential rivals.

Constantine couldn't tolerate other people's popularity, and there was one man whom the masses loved and wanted to see on the throne. The emperor had him killed too, under false accusations. The unfortunate man was named Crispus, and he was the emperor's oldest son.

No matter how hard he tried, Constantine couldn't keep everything under control. He had many issues with the church. Even though he had the means to influence the official doctrine established in Nicaea, the opinions and faith of his subjects were beyond his power. Arius and other heretics gained the support of people who did not care whether those priests were banished from the church. Even Constantine himself was never completely sure which faction within the church he should support. Disinterested in theological speculation, he only wanted to back up the most popular one so that it would help him spread his influence. It seems that near the end of his life he thought the Arians would win, so when he was finally baptized, it was an Arian bishop who performed the ceremony.

Chapter 12 – Constantinian Dynasty

Constantine was one of the most competent rulers in Roman history, but he was still far from perfect. Some issues that he left unsolved became major problems after he died. The old Roman religion persisted along with Christianity. This model of religious tolerance worked well under Constantine, but now it threatened to break the empire apart. The other unsolved issue was the one of succession.

Constantine's Sons

Constantine was so concerned about his own position that he arranged the execution of his most skilled heir, as we saw in the previous chapter. The three sons that survived, named Constantine II, Constantius II, and Constans, split the empire among themselves and immediately started fighting each other in order to take the whole. After a couple of years of civil war, Constantius II emerged victoriously. But the empire had many enemies that grew stronger year after year, and he wasn't able to be present at all frontiers at the same time. He desperately needed someone from his family to lead the rest of the army, but he had expediently killed them all. Well, almost all, as there was a nerdy little cousin Julian whom Constantius spared because the boy didn't seem to be much of a threat. The emperor would think differently, had he only known what potential young Julian had.

Julian the Apostate

Flavius Claudius Julianus (later known as Julian the Apostate) spent his childhood imprisoned in his home, reading the Greek and Roman classics, as a child. He had never shown any ambitions other than intellectual ones, and when he turned 19, he was easily granted the permission to travel and pursue his studies of the classical world. During his journeys from Pergamum to Ephesus, Julian studied philosophy, rejected Christianity, and embraced Neoplatonism. He never told anyone—especially his Christian teachers—about his apostasy and joining a pagan movement because he didn't want to compromise the privileges that he enjoyed.

But the moment had come when he could no longer continue his life as a scholar. Constantius needed him to lead an imperial army and deal with enemies on the northern frontier, as the emperor himself had to fight Persia. So, he made Julian his Caesar (junior emperor), gave him 360 men (who, according to Julian's words, "knew only how to pray"[xxxiii]), and directed him to Gaul.

Julian had zero military experience. In the eyes of others, he was just a shy scholar. Yet in the five years he spent in Gaul, he showed incredible results. Julian organized the local army and made it efficient, then pushed out the barbarians, and set dozens of thousands of war prisoners free. When he established peace in the province, he pursued and crushed the Germanic tribes in their own terrain, imprisoned their king, and sent him to Constantinople in chains.

Constantius was instantly petrified. His young cousin was powerful and people admired him. To discourage Julian, the emperor demanded money and men from Gaul to be sent to him as a help against the Persians.

Julian's men did not want to abandon their homes and join Constantius's army on the east, so one night they gathered around Julian's palace, hailed him as their emperor, and asked him to lead them against Constantius. Julian felt Zeus was on his side, and he gladly said yes. He no longer had to pretend he was Christian, and he sent instructions to all Roman cities to restore Roman religion.

Julian didn't have to fight Constantius, who died of an illness in the meantime. As his only heir, the new emperor Julian simply arrived in Constantinople, where he was hailed wholeheartedly by the crowds as well as the Senate.

Restoring Graeco-Roman Culture: Julian's Futile Dreams

Julian wasn't completely content with his new status. The strength of the empire had declined considerably over the ages. He saw degeneration, greed, moral decay, and a lack of discipline everywhere. The emperor had a clear idea of the causes of such a decline: it all happened because of Christianity. The new faith glorified 'feminine' attributes such as kindness and forgiveness, at the expense of the long-established Roman sense of honor and duty.

Julian knew that persecution wouldn't produce the results that he wanted. So he decided to adopt Constantine's strategy, but for an opposite cause—the restoration of old customs and religions that were now considered pagan. Julian published an edict of toleration, which contained a small clause which stated that Roman paganism was a superior religion. Temples throughout the empire were open again, and everything was set up, but the populace had already acknowledged Christ as their true God and wasn't willing to abandon the new hope. No matter how hard the emperor tried to reverse the course of history, nothing seemed to work. Then he remembered how Constantine made Christianity dominant overnight—he fought at the Milvian Bridge and won, stating that Christ had led him. The next step was clear: Julian had to emerge glorious in a decisive battle, and people should be informed that Mars and Jupiter (or the Greek Ares and Zeus) led their emperor.

Julian the Apostate[xxxiv]

Julian prepared for the key victory in a traditional Graeco-Roman way by asking the oracle at Delphi for a prophecy. But the words of the oracle were disappointing: "Tell the emperor that my hall has fallen to the ground. Phoibos no longer has his house, nor his mantic bay, nor his prophetic spring; the water has dried up." [xxxv]

The emperor made several other attempts to prove that ancient gods were real and on his side, while the Christian God was an impostor. According to a biblical prophecy, the ancient Jewish temple in Jerusalem couldn't be rebuilt until the end times. So Julian decided to rebuild the temple and prove it all a lie. But he didn't manage to do it. He made two attempts, and each of them ended with a catastrophe. First it was an earthquake, and the second time it was a fire that burned the entire structure to the ground.

These futile attempts made Julian increasingly unpopular, mainly because he needed means to achieve them, and he used the gold from a Christian cathedral to pay his army.

Finally, in 363, he marched to Persia with his impressive army. They entered the Persian land without difficulty, but it was impossible to get across high walls and break into the Persian capital of Ctesiphon. A long siege was out of the question, as the Romans couldn't stand the heat. On top of that, a large Persian army was on its way to defend the capital. Disappointed, Julian decided to abandon the siege. Then in a couple of months, the Persians attacked the eastern frontier, and Julian instantly received a fatal wound. He died as the last pagan Roman Emperor and the last emperor from the Constantinian dynasty.

Chapter 13 – Decline and Fall of the Western Roman Empire

The world was changing rapidly, and Rome was soon to fall into the hands of Germanic leaders. Germanic tribes had been trying to invade Roman land for ages, without success. This time it was different; they came in peace, as settlers who sought refuge from the new frightening force—the Huns. Nevertheless, the newcomers weren't eager to adapt and embrace the Roman culture. As a result, Roman society was changing forever, in a way that was not beneficial to the Romans. On top of that, the empire was governed by one incompetent emperor after another.[xxxvi]

Valentinian, Valens, and Gratian

The emperor that succeeded Julian died an unheroic death: a brazier was left burning in his tent overnight and he suffocated. His sons, Valentinian and Valens, split the empire again. Valentinian took the West and Valens became the ruler of Roman East. After eleven years, Valentinian died and his son Gratian succeeded him, but he was too inexperienced and under the influence of his uncle Valens.

Valens made a seemingly favorable arrangement with the two hundred thousand Visigoth and Ostrogoth migrants who wanted to stay in the Roman territory. The settlers would be given properties in

Thrace, and their men would become Roman soldiers. But it did not end well. The hostility between the natives and the novices intensified. In 378, Valens and Gratian were compelled to attack the Goths near Adrianople. They lacked a proper plan and genuine collaboration, and the action turned out to be a catastrophe. The long walk and heat drained the Romans, and the Goths easily slew two-thirds of them. Now every barbaric tribe could enter the Roman territory and do whatever they wanted. The Goths spread east and menaced Constantinople. It looked like there was no way out.

Theodosius

Valens died in a skirmish, but the East was not without an emperor for long. Western emperor Gratian chose his best general, Theodosius, and made him the emperor of the eastern half of the empire. Theodosius had a truly difficult task to find some fresh blood to replace tens of thousands of experienced soldiers that had been slaughtered at the Adrianople disaster. Now everyone—including the barbarians—had to serve in the army. The arrangement he made was similar to the one made by Valens, but Theodosius paid more attention to the details. It worked well for a while, although it left damaging consequences that would become obvious in a few decades and would result in the collapse of the Western Roman Empire.

Exclusiveness of Christianity

In 382 Theodosius fell ill, and he thought he was about to die. Just like Constantine before him, the eastern emperor wanted to be baptized before he expired. However, after the ceremony, he miraculously recovered. This experience prompted him to change the way he ruled the empire. Killing innocents was now impossible, and he no longer could ignore the disputes within the church.

Theodosius banned both the Arian heresy and paganism within the empire. Incited by his religious mentor, Bishop Ambrose of Milan, he closed the public temples, renounced the title of Pontifex

Maximus (the chief priest of the traditional Roman religion), and outlawed all things pagan. The Olympic Games, the Delphic Oracle, the Temple of Vesta, and the eternal fire were now history. Eventually, in 391, Theodosius officially announced Christianity as the only religion in the empire.

The Sack of Rome

Theodosius's descendants lacked the capacity to deal with the 'barbaric' forces in the empire, and those tribes enlarged their influence. Generals—who more often than not had a barbaric origin—enjoyed greater influence than emperors. This was particularly obvious in the western part of the empire, where Emperor Honorius was effectively in the shadow of General Stilicho. Ironically, Stilicho was an outstanding commander, yet neither the elite in Rome nor Constantinople supported him. On one occasion, he tried to bribe the Visigothic King Alaric because he realized fighting him would be detrimental. Stilicho's enemies then convinced Emperor Honorius that he had betrayed Rome, and the emperor had him killed. Italy was virtually defenseless, and in 401, Alaric's army simply entered Italy and sacked Rome. Honorius escaped to Ravenna, leaving the citizens to fend for themselves.

The Horrifying Huns

Shocked by the sack of Rome, the new emperor of the East, Theodosius II, built massive walls around Constantinople. Alaric did not have a chance to try to invade the New Rome, but others did, including the mighty Attila the Hun and his menacing army. Constantinople remained unharmed, but Rome was utterly exposed. At first, Attila accepted payment in order to leave the Romans alone, and so he did. A few months later, Honorius's sister Honoria was pressed into a marriage with an unpleasant senator. Desperately trying to avoid the wedding, she sent a letter and a ring to Attila. The powerful Hun then returned to take what was his. Surprisingly, the Huns did not ruin the city. Pope Leo—the only public official who was still in Roma at this point—persuaded him to leave immediately. The next morning, Attila's men found their leader dead in his tent.

Resisting Barbarian Masters

Attila now expired, the Huns no longer presented a threat to the Roman Empire. However, the true enemy was still present and had immense power. The barbarians were not only integrated into the society; they were just behind the throne, effectively controlling the emperors. When Emperor Valentinian III tried to put an end to it and get rid of his barbarian master, he was murdered too. The emperor's widow then called for the Vandals to come and help Romans. They arrived, pillaged Rome, and took the unwise empress with them to Carthage.

In Constantinople, Emperor Leo wanted to resist the Sarmatian general Aspar – who effectively ruled that part of the empire- but also avoid ending up like his western colleague. Leo found a way to take the military control from him and give it to another general, Tarasicodissa the Isaurian. They charged Aspar with treason, and Tarasicodissa—now Hellenized and named Zeno—was married to Leo's daughter.

Leo was an ambitious emperor, and he wanted to subjugate the Vandal kingdom of North Africa. He equipped the army well but made a colossal mistake with the choice of the commander in charge. He chose his brother-in-law Basiliscus, who soon proved to be among the most incapable generals in history. He landed too far from Carthage, accidentally wrecked the fleet, panicked, and fled, leaving the devastated army behind. Interestingly, Basiliscus believed he was competent to rule the empire. Leo chose Zeno as his heir. Basiliscus caused him some trouble by overthrowing him, but the people were on Zeno's side, and the better man won the throne.

The West Falls. The East Moves On.

Zeno worked diligently to re-establishing stability in the Eastern Roman Empire, but the West was doomed. In 476, a barbarian general named Odoacer got bored by all the pretending and puppet-emperors, and he sent the teenage Emperor Romulus Augustulus into exile. The barbarian ruler wasn't interested in taking the title of Roman emperor, and he took the crown and scepter and sent them as a gesture of good will to Zeno.

The Eastern Emperor wasn't happy to give Odoacer support, but he couldn't afford to fight him at that moment. Eventually, he came up with a brilliant idea and solved two problems at once. The Ostrogoth King Theodoric was making a mess in the Balkans, and Zeno couldn't fight him. So he gave him the authority to rule the West. The Goths collectively moved to Italy and overthrew Odoacer. Rome wasn't Roman anymore. The Eastern Empire, on the other hand, finally became free from barbaric influence. Zeno was successful in restoring stability but didn't live long enough to witness the bright new era that began thanks to him.

Chapter 14 – The Byzantine Millennium

The city of Constantinople was founded during the chaotic third century when revolts and civil wars were normal, and Roman emperors merely lasted for a year. Under Constantine, the new city had become the capital of the whole Roman Empire. Now that the Western Roman Empire ceased to exist, the Eastern Empire was the only one. Today it is widely known as the Byzantine Empire, but at the time when these events took place, it was formally known as the Eastern Roman Empire. The citizens of the eastern capital and its rulers saw themselves as Romans. Everybody else, including their enemies, considered them Roman as well. When Constantinople fell to the Ottomans, the Sultan Mehmed II took the title Caesar of Rome. But that happened in the fifteenth century, in the period that could not be named "ancient" by any stretch of thoughts. We'll address it though, because of its continuity with the ancient Roman world. As for now, our story continues with the most glorious Byzantine emperor and his controversial wife.

Justinian and Theodora

Justinian had been truly powerful years before he became emperor. Born as Peter Sabbatius, this promising young man changed his name to Justinian out of the gratitude he felt toward his uncle Justin, who happened to be the emperor at the time. Justin not only adopted his nephew and helped him receive elite education, he also listened to his advice and allowed him to make strategically important decisions. The elderly emperor even gave Justinian his consent when he decided to marry "a lady of the stage" named Theodora.

Justinian helped the neighboring peoples to deal with their oppressive masters. Representatives from numerous states gathered in Constantinople, and the city practically became the center of the world. The vassal kings that had been obliged to serve the king of Persia happily changed sides, empowered by the support from the empire and Justinian. Besides, the troops led by Justinian's bodyguard, Belisarius, overtook Armenia from the Persians. This was just the beginning for the visionary emperor.

The Coronation of Justinian and Theodora in Hagia Sofia was spectacular, and it anticipated an age of splendor. Indeed, his reign is now considered the golden age in Byzantine history, thanks to his military achievements and magnificent construction projects. In addition to that, he produced the first ever written codex of Roman law. Unfortunately, the people were not very happy because he also raised taxes. That's why he almost got killed in the Nika revolt, when 30,000 people raised against him at the Hippodrome. The revolt was suppressed and the rioters slaughtered by Belisarius's army. No one ever questioned Justinian's decisions again.

One God in Heaven, One Emperor on Earth

Justinian believed the Roman Empire was not complete without the city of Rome and that it was his duty to restore the heavenly order, liberate Rome, and reunite the church. Luckily for the emperor, he had the finest general in Roman history at his disposal. Although hugely outnumbered, the army led by Belisarius defeated the Vandals in Africa and reconquered Carthage. After that, with only 5,000 men he retook Rome and all of Italy. He might have been able to reconquer Spain and the rest of Western Europe if only the empress had not feared that Belisarius was too powerful to be trusted.

Later years brought plague and famine. After all was over, Justinian managed to uphold relative prosperity and peace for the rest of his life. No Roman Emperor spoke Latin as his first language after Justinian, and very few were such visionaries in the whole of Roman history.[xxxvii]

For the rest of its long history, the Eastern Roman Empire had its ups and downs. One of the greatest challenges was the aggressive expansion of Muslim tribes, which able Byzantine generals fought numerous times. Even in times of greatest crisis, Constantinople was well protected and unapproachable for its enemies. The official language was Greek, and the dominant religion was Eastern Orthodox Christianity. Despite being a religious society, its educational system was remarkably secular. Its cultural life flourished, and the elites of the surrounding peoples were educated at the University of Constantinople, where they learned mathematics, rhetoric, languages, and law. The Dark Ages never entered Byzantium. Constantinople was the shield of light and civilization in Medieval Europe and beyond.[xxxviii] Moreover, the Eastern Empire guarded the rest of Europe against swiftly expanding Islamic forces.[xxxix]

The Crusades

The dominance of Byzantium lasted for more than a millennium, but eventually it came to an end. Ironically, the first damage made to Constantinople did not come from the hands of Muslims. The city that had not been conquered before was eventually sacked and burned by fellow Christians during the Fourth Crusade.

The trouble began in the eleventh century, during the advancement of Seljuk Turks who invaded the imperial territory in order to stay there. The Byzantine elite was so corrupt at the time that they betrayed the emperor Romanus Diogenes in a decisive moment during a battle against the Seljuks, only because they did not want a strong emperor who could limit their privileges. Like centuries ago in ancient times, the empire was now tormented by civil wars.

Eventually, in 1081, a man with potential was crowned. It was the general Alexius Comnenus.

By this point, the Orthodox and Catholic churches were separated and not in good terms. Nevertheless, Alexius wrote to Pope Urban asking for support against the Saracens. That's how the crusades began.

The first crusaders that arrived were an undisciplined bunch led by Peter the Hermit. On the way to Constantinople, they set fire to many towns, and when they arrived, they killed a number of Greeks in Asia Minor. Finally, the Turks crushed them. The next crusades were more successful in their mission, as they won several battles against the Turks and entered Jerusalem. Still, they presented a much bigger danger to the striking city of Constantinople than to the Muslims. The Fourth Crusade never reached its holy destination. The knights and peasants entered Constantinople. The Duke of Venice, who had some unresolved issues with the Byzantine elite, told the crusaders that the Greeks were heretics. As a result, they ruined the city and took all the treasure they could find, including reliquaries from the tombs and the ornaments from the churches. In the end, they burned the city.

After being condemned by Pope Innocent, the crusaders decided to stay and create the Latin Empire of Constantinople. The genuine Byzantine elite and the new emperor were located in Nicaea, and they undermined the Latins with various diplomatic activities until one day emperor Michael Palaeologus gathered an army, entered Constantinople, and made the Latins panic and run away.

The Ottomans

A group of Turkish warriors led by a man named Osman conquered all other cities in the empire, and now they aimed at Constantinople. The city's defenses could buy time, but they weren't that unbreakable anymore. The emperor Manuel II asked support from the West, but no one came. The tension lasted for several decades, during which the Ottomans suffered some setbacks and left the Byzantines alone for a while.

Finally, in 1453, the Turkish Sultan Mehmed II the Conqueror, armed with modern cannons, opened fire on the city walls. The offensive lasted for 48 days. Finally, the Turkish army backed up by elite troops called the Janissaries entered the city from the sea. Many citizens gathered in Hagia Sophia, waiting for an angel to save them. They were all killed. It was the end of Roman history.

Hagia Sophia today (adapted into a mosque), Istanbul, Turkey[xl]

The Timeline of Roman History

Ancient History: the Roman Republic

753 BC	Foundation of Rome
509 BC	Overthrow of the Roman monarchy
494 BC	First secession of plebs
445 BC	The legalization of marriage between patricians and plebeians
396 BC	Roman soldiers earned a salary for the first time
366 BC	The first plebeian consul held office
351 BC	The first plebeian dictator and censor were elected
343-41 BC	The First Samnite War
340-38 BC	Latin (Social) War
337 BC	The first plebeian Praetor was elected
328-304 BC	The Second Samnite War
287 BC	Conflict of the Orders: the first secession of plebs
280-272 BC	Pyrrhic War

241 BC province of Sicilia	First Punic War: Sicily was organized as the
218 BC departed Cartagena	Second Punic War: A Carthaginian army
216 BC	Battle of Cannae
214-205 BC	First Macedonian War
204-201 BC	Second Punic War
200-192 BC	Second Macedonian War
188 BC	Roman–Seleucid War:
149-146 BC	Third Punic War
133 BC Gracchus	Murder of the Tribune of the Plebs Tiberius
112 BC	Jugurthine War
107 BC	Gaius Marius was elected consul
91-88 BC	Social War
88 BC	Sulla's first civil war
83-82 BC	Sulla's second civil war
63 BC	Pompey conquered Jerusalem; Cicero was elected consul; Catilinarian conspiracy
59 BC	The First Triumvirate
58 -50 BC	Gallic Wars: Roman forces barred the westward migration of the Helvetii across the Rhône
49 BC	Caesar illegally crossed the Rubicon
44 BC	Assassination of Julius Caesar
43 BC	The Second Triumvirate of Augustus, Mark Antony and Marcus Aemilius Lepidus

42 BC	Liberators' civil war: Augustus and Antony led some thirty legions to northern Greece in pursuit of Caesar's assassins
33 BC	The Second Triumvirate expired
31 BC	Battle of Actium
30 BC	Final War of the Roman Republic: Antony's forces defected to Augustus. Antony and Cleopatra committed suicide

Early Empire

27 BC	The Senate granted Augustus the titles Augustus, majestic, and Princeps, first
21 BC	Augustus married his daughter Julia to his general Marcus Vipsanius Agrippa
12 BC	Agrippa died of fever
11 BC	Augustus married Julia to Tiberius
9 BC	Nero Claudius Drusus died from injuries sustained falling from a horse
6 BC	Augustus offered Tiberius tribunician power and imperium over the eastern half of the Empire. Tiberius refused, announcing his retirement to Rhodes
2 BC	Augustus was acclaimed Pater Patriae, father of the country, by the Senate; Augustus convicted Julia of adultery and treason and exiled her with her mother Scribonia to Ventotene
AD 4	Augustus adopted Tiberius as his son and granted him tribunician power

AD 13 as co-princeps	Tiberius was granted power equal to Augustus
AD 14	Augustus died
AD 16	Battle of the Weser River: A Roman army led by Germanicus decisively defeated a Germanic force on the Weser
AD 18	Tiberius granted Germanicus imperium over the eastern half of the Empire
AD 19	Germanicus died in Antioch, possibly after being poisoned on Tiberius's orders
AD 37	Tiberius died, and his will left his offices jointly to Caligula and Drusus Julius Caesar's son, his grandson Tiberius Gemellus
AD 41	Caligula was assassinated by the centurion Cassius Chaerea; The Praetorian Guard acclaimed Nero Claudius Drusus's son Claudius princeps
AD 43	Roman conquest of Britain
AD 49	Claudius married Agrippina the Younger
AD 50	Claudius adopted Agrippina's son Nero
AD 54	Claudius died after being poisoned by Agrippina, and Nero succeeded him as princeps
AD 64	Great Fire of Rome
AD 66	First Jewish–Roman War: The Jewish population of Judea revolted against Roman rule
AD 68	The Senate declared Nero an enemy of the state, and he orders his secretary Epaphroditos to kill him; the Senate accepted Galba,

governor of Hispania Tarraconensis, as ruler of Rome

AD 69   The Praetorian Guard assassinated Galba and acclaimed Otho ruler of Rome; Vitellius defeated Otho; The Senate recognized Vespasian as ruler of Rome

AD 70   Siege of Jerusalem: The Roman general Titus breached the walls of Jerusalem, sacked the city and destroyed the Second Temple

AD 71   Roman conquest of Britain: Roman forces entered modern Scotland

AD 79   Vespasian died. He was succeeded by his son Titus

AD 80   Rome was partially destroyed by fire; the Colosseum was completed

AD 81   Titus died of fever, and his younger brother Domitian succeeded him

AD 96   Domitian was assassinated by members of the royal household; Nerva was declared ruler of Rome by the Senate

AD 97   Nerva adopted the general and former consul Trajan as his son

AD 98   Nerva died, and Trajan succeeded him

AD 117   Trajan died, and the Senate accepted the general Hadrian as ruler of Rome

AD 132-135   Bar Kokhba revolt in Judea

AD 138   Hadrian adopted Antoninus Pius as his son and successor; Hadrian died, probably from heart failure. Antoninus succeeded him

AD 161 succeeded him	Antoninus died; Marcus and Lucius Verus
AD 165-180	Antonine Plague
AD 169 the sole ruler of Rome	Lucius Verus died of disease, leaving Marcus
AD 177 ruler with himself	Marcus named his natural son Commodus co-
AD 180	Marcus died
AD 192	Commodus was strangled to death

The Late Empire

284	Roman forces in the east elected the consul Diocletian their ruler and proclaimed him augustus.
285	Diocletian gave Maximian the title Caesar
286	Diocletian proclaimed Maximian augustus of the west, ruling himself as augustus of the east
293	Diocletian established the Tetrarchy, appointing Constantius Chlorus to hold the office of Caesar under Maximian in the west and Galerius to hold the title under himself in the east
301	Diocletian issued the Edict on Maximum Prices, reforming the currency and setting price ceilings on a number of goods
303	Diocletianic Persecution
305	Diocletian and Maximian abdicated. Constantius and Galerius were elevated to augusti in the west and east; Galerius

	appointed Flavius Valerius Severus Caesar in the west and Maximinus II Caesar in the east
306	Constantius died at Eboracum; his troops acclaimed his son Constantine the Great augustus
306-312	Civil wars of the Tetrarchy
312	Battle of the Milvian Bridge
313	Constantine the Great and Licinius issued the Edict of Milan, providing for restitution to Christians injured during the persecutions
324	Battle of Adrianople
325	First Council of Nicaea
326 oldest son Crispus	Constantine the Great ordered the death of his
330	Constantine the Great moved his capital to Byzantium and renamed the city Constantinople, the city of Constantine
337 succeeded him	Constantine the Great died; his sons
355	Constantius II declared Julian (emperor) Caesar and granted him command in Gaul
357	Battle of Strasbourg: Julian defeated a vastly superior Alemanni force near Argentoratum, solidifying Roman control west of the Rhine
360	The Petulantes, ordered east from Paris in preparation for a war with the Sasanian Empire, instead mutinied and proclaimed Julian augustus
361 Julian	Constantius II died of fever; succeeded by

364	The army acclaimed the general Valentinian I the Great augustus; Valentinian the Great appointed his younger brother Valens augustus with rule over the eastern Empire, and continued as augustus in the west
375	Valentinian the Great died of a stroke his son Gratian, then junior augustus in the west, succeeded him as senior augustus.
378	Battle of Adrianople: A combined Gothic-Alanic force decisively defeated the Roman army near Edirne; Valens was killed.
379	Gratian named the general Theodosius I the Great augustus in the east
380	Theodosius the Great issued the Edict of Thessalonica, making Christianity the state church of the Roman Empire
395	Theodosius the Great died; his elder son Arcadius succeeded him as augustus in the eastern Byzantine Empire; the young Honorius became sole augustus in the Western Roman Empire under the regency of Magister militum Stilicho
398	Gildonic War: Gildo, comes from Africa, was killed following a failed rebellion against the Western Roman Empire
402	Ravenna becomes the capital of the Western Roman Empire
410	The Visigoths sacked Rome under their king Alaric I
424	The Byzantine augustus Theodosius II the Younger, the Calligrapher named the young

	Valentinian III, his cousin and Constantius III's son, Caesar with rule over the west; his mother Galla Placidia was appointed a regent
447	Battle of the Utus: The Huns under Attila defeated a Byzantine army in a bloody battle near the Vit
457	The Byzantine augustus Leo I the Thracian appointed Majorian Magister militum in the west
468	Battle of Cap Bon: The Vandal Kingdom destroyed a combined Western Roman and Byzantine invasion fleet at Cap Bon
474	Leo the Thracian died; his grandson Leo II succeeded him. Zeno became co-augustus of the Byzantine Empire with his young son Leo II
475	Basiliscus, brother of Leo the Thracian's widow Verina, was acclaimed augustus of the Byzantine Empire by the Byzantine Senate
476	Zeno recaptured Constantinople and accepted Basiliscus's surrender; Germanic foederati renounced Western Roman authority; Odoacer conquered the Western Roman capital Ravenna, forced Romulus to abdicate and declared himself king of Italy; the Senate sent Zeno the imperial regalia of the Western Roman Empire

The Byzantine Empire

527	Augustus Justin I appointed his older son Justinian I the Great co-augustus with himself; Justin I died

529	The Codex Justinianus, which attempted to consolidate and reconcile contradictions in Roman law, was promulgated
532	Justinian the Great ordered the construction of the Hagia Sophia in Constantinople
533-534	Vandalic War: A Byzantine force under the general Belisarius departed for the Vandal Kingdom
535-554	Gothic War (535–554): Byzantine forces crossing from Africa invaded Sicily and Rome
537	The Hagia Sophia was completed
565	Belisarius died; Justinian the Great died
602-628	Byzantine–Sasanian War of 602–628
634	Muslim conquest of the Levant
640	Muslim conquest of Egypt
641	Siege of Alexandria (641): Byzantine authorities in the Egyptian capital Alexandria surrendered to the besieging Rashidun army
663	Basileus Constans II visited Rome
698	Battle of Carthage (698): An Umayyad siege and blockade of Carthage forced the retreat of Byzantine forces; the city was conquered and destroyed
730	Basileus Leo III the Isaurian promulgated an edict forbidding the veneration of religious images, beginning the first Byzantine Iconoclasm
787	Second Council of Nicaea: An ecumenical council in Nicaea ended which endorsed the

	veneration of images, ending the first Byzantine Iconoclasm
1002	Byzantine conquest of Bulgaria
1054	East-West Schism: The papal legate Humbert of Silva Candida laid on the altar of Hagia Sophia a document proclaiming the excommunication of Michael I Cerularius, the patriarch of Constantinople
1071	Battle of Manzikert: A Seljuk force decisively defeated the Byzantine Empire near Malazgirt; the basileus Romanos IV Diogenes was captured
1081	Nikephoros III Botaneiates was deposed and replaced as basileus by Alexios I Komnenos
1098	The First Crusader leader Bohemond I declared himself Prince of Antioch
1204	Siege of Constantinople: Fourth Crusaders breached and sacked Constantinople, deposed the basileus Alexios V Doukas and established the Latin Empire under their leader Baldwin I, as Latin Emperor
1261	Michael VIII Palaiologos conquered Constantinople and was crowned basileus in Constantinople along with his infant son Andronikos II Palaiologos
1326-1453	Byzantine-Ottoman Wars
1453	Fall of Constantinople: Ottoman forces entered Constantinople; Basileus Constantine XI Palaiologos was killed

End Notes

[i] The title of the book on the Byzantine Empire by Lars Brownsworth

[ii] Livy [Titus Livius (59 BC–17 AD) – a Roman historian; his history of Rome from its foundation to his own time contained 142 books, of which 35 survive] points to the link between the word wolf and a colloquial expression used for a prostitute and believes it was the former who took care of the baby brothers

[iii] As referred by Beard (*SPQR, A History of Ancient Rome*)

[iv] The age and origin of the figures is a subject of controversy. The Lupa was long thought to be an Etruscan work of the 5th century BC, with the twins added in the late 15th century AD, but radiocarbon and thermoluminescence dating has found that it was possibly manufactured in the 13th century AD.

[v] "So perish anyone else who shall leap over my walls!" screamed Romulus upon killing his brother. (Livy)

[vi] David M. Gwynn, *The Roman Republic: A Very Short Introduction,* Oxford University Press, 2012

[vii] Plutarch, *Moralia, On the fortune of the Romans*
http://www.gutenberg.org/ebooks/23639

[viii] Beard

[ix] Ibid.

[x] Gwynn

[xi] Stephen P. Oakley, "The Early Republic," in *The Cambridge Companion to the Roman Republic*, edited by Harriet I. Flower, Cambridge University Press, 2006.

[xii] These walls were mistakenly said to have been built by Servius Tullius and are still known as the "Servian Walls."

[xiii] Livy

[xiv] Octavius's family was from Thurii, hence the addition of the name Thurinus.

[xv] Bust of the emperor with the Civic Crown, Palace Bevilacqua, Verona, Italy / Wikimedia Commons.

[xvi] Publius (or Gaius) Cornelius Tacitus, Annales (The Annals).

xvii Gaius Suetonius Tranquillus, The Twelve Caesars: The Life of Tiberius.

xviii Suetonius, The Lives of Twelve Caesars, Life of Nero and Cassius Dio, Roman History.

xix Tacitus, *Histories*.

xx Portrait of Nero. Marble, Roman artwork, 1st century AD. From the Augustan area on the Palatine Hill. Antiquarium of the Palatine; source: Wikimedia Commons.

xxi Suetonius, Cassius Dio, Pliny the Elder.

xxii Ibid.

xxiii Brian W. Jones, *The Emperor Domitian*, 1993.

xxiv Machiavelli, *Discourses on Livy.*

xxv Michael Peachin, "Rome the Superpower: 96–235 CE," in: *A companion to the Roman Empire* edited by David Potter, Blackwell Publishing Ltd, 2006.

xxvi Wikimedia Commons.

xxvii Cassius Dio, *Roman History*.

xxviii Refer to chapter 5.

xxix Julian Bennett, *Trajan*. Optimus Princeps. Bloomington: Indiana University Press, 2001..

xxx Scriptores Historiae Augustae, Hadrian.

xxxi Ibid.

xxxii Cassius Dio.

xxxiii Julian, as cited by Brownworth.

xxxiv Image courtesy of Classical Numismatic Group/Wikipedia Commons.

xxxv As cited on
https://en.wikipedia.org/wiki/List_of_oracular_statements_from_Delphi; five different translations available here:
http://laudatortemporisacti.blogspot.com/2012/12/the-last-oracle.html.

xxxvi Gibbon.

xxxvii Brownworth.

xxxviii Lars Brownworth, *Lost to the West: The Forgotten Byzantine Empire That Rescued Western Civilization*, Crown Publishing, New York, 2009.

xxxix Brownworth; Edward Gibbon, *The History Of The Decline And Fall Of The Roman Empire*, Vol. Five, Project Gutenberg edition:
http://www.gutenberg.org/files/735/735-h/735-h.htm.

xl Image courtesy of Arild Vågen (Wikipedia Commons).

Free Bonus from Captivating History (Available for a Limited time)

Hi History Lovers!

Now you have a chance to join our exclusive history list so you can get your first history ebook for free as well as discounts and a potential to get more history books for free! Simply visit the link below to join.

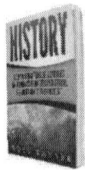

Captivatinghistory.com/ebook

Also, make sure to follow us on:

Twitter: @Captivhistory

Facebook: Captivating History:@captivatinghistory

29188160R00054

Printed in Great Britain
by Amazon